Estate Planning for Authors: Your Final Letter (and why you need to write it now)

a Strategies for Success guide
by
M. L. Buchman

Buchman Bookworks

Other works by M.L. Buchman

Strategies for Success: (NF)
Manaaging Your Inner Artist / Writer
Estate Planning for Authors

Where Dreams
Where Dreams are Born
Where Dreams Reside
Where Dreams Are of Christmas
Where Dreams Unfold
Where Dreams Are Written

Eagle Cove
Return to Eagle Cove
Recipe for Eagle Cove
Longing for Eagle Cove
Keepsake for Eagle Cove

Henderson's Ranch
Nathan's Big Sky

The Night Stalkers

MAIN FLIGHT
The Night Is Mine
I Own the Dawn
Wait Until Dark
Take Over at Midnight
Light Up the Night
Bring On the Dusk
By Break of Day

WHITE HOUSE HOLIDAY
Daniel's Christmas

Frank's Independence Day
Peter's Christmas
Zachary's Christmas
Roy's Independence Day
Damien's Christmas

AND THE NAVY
Christmas at Steel Beach
Christmas at Peleliu Cove

5E
Target of the Heart
Target Lock on Love
Target of Mine

Delta Force
Target Engaged
Heart Strike

Dead Chef Thrillers
Swap Out!
One Chef!
Two Chef!

Firehawks

MAIN FLIGHT
Pure Heat
Full Blaze
Hot Point
Flash of Fire
Wild Fire

SMOKEJUMPERS
Wildfire at Dawn

Wildfire at Larch Creek
Wildfire on the Skagit

Deities Anonymous
Cookbook from Hell: Reheated
Saviors 101

SF/F Titles
The Nara Reaction
Monk's Maze
the Me and Elsie Chronicles

Get a free Starter Library at:
www.mlbuchman.com

Don't Miss a Thing!

Sign up for M. L. Buchman's newsletter
today
and receive:
Release News
Free Short Stories
a Free Starter Library

Do it today. Do it now.

Contents

Dedication

To my wife and daughter, I hope this helps.
It's the best I know how to protect you both.

My Thanks
To those who have listened, suggested, read,
commented, prodded, and pushed until this
book came to life: Kristine Kathryn Rusch, Dean
Wesley Smith, Leah Cutter, Blaze Ward, Suzanne
Brockmann, and the attendees of multiple
workshops whose questions so accelerated my
learning curve. I couldn't have done it without
every one of you.

Purpose of this book

Your Will states who gets what.

Your *Final Letter* tells them what they can, and should, do with it once they have it.

This book is about the second bit. It suggests a method to write a "Final Letter" that will organize your literary estate and educate your heirs. Or, if the creator behind the estate didn't write one, this book can act as a guide for their heirs to understand what options exist to manage a literary estate.

Disclaimer

I am not a lawyer, nor (as a friend of mine is fond of saying) do I play one on TV. Nothing in this book should be construed as legal advice.

However, I have:

- 30 years' experience as a project manager.
- 9 years of that were in law as a paralegal, computer systems designer, and eventually project manager of multiple multimillion dollar, class action settlements including some of the largest settlements in the 2000s.
- 20+ years as a publishing professional.
- I've also spent over a year researching this material, presenting it several times for writers (some of whom *are* Intellectual Property or IP lawyers), and incorporating their feedback each time.

Part I: Getting Started

Introduction

So, what is this book? This is about how I developed the letter I wrote for my wife and kid. A letter that explained how they could manage my intellectual property once I'm gone.

How many of your heirs even know what *intellectual property* means in that last sentence, never mind the options that exist regarding how to manage it? We need to educate our heirs and do it in simple language—I will repeat this often and it still won't be often enough.

Dear Heir, Intellectual Property (commonly referred to as IP), which we'll get into more later, is all the stuff the author created:

books, stories, notes, audio, film, plays, and potentially much more.

This book is first an education that I gave myself and then it is about the method I've found to communicate this to my heirs. Further along I've included a copy of my own Final Letter as well as a list of the best reference books I've found so far in my research.

The Heir

When I say "heir," this may be as simple as "my wife" or as complex as a corporation operated in trust for multiple generations of descendants, friends, and charities. For most of this book, that differentiation won't matter and I'll be clear when it does. For simplicity I will refer to heir or heirs to encompass all of these different variations.

> *Dear Heir, You can also use this book as a guide to help the creator of the literary estate organize their estate—to make your life easier in the future. Maybe you can use the story below to nudge them into action.*

The Inside Story: Elvis Presley
Elvis Presley left $500,000 to his ex-wife

Priscilla and the remainder of his estate to his daughter Lisa Marie.

Generous? Not very.

The balance of the estate was worth only another $500,000. Still not bad—except that it was incurring over $500,000 per year in expenses. Nine-year-old Lisa Marie was going to be bankrupt before she was ten.

Priscilla stepped in on behalf of her daughter. She didn't need the money, she was already a successful businesswoman worth several million in her own right. But she wanted to help her daughter. After years of massive lawsuits that are a matter of public record, Priscilla recovered control of the mismanaged estate and then ran it properly.

Did she succeed? The Elvis Presley estate is worth over $400 million dollars as of 2017 and he is still a household name forty years after his death.

Lesson: If you leave your estate in a mess, will there be a Priscilla to clean it up? Or will your literary legacy die shortly after you do because the tangled disaster you left behind was too much of a pain in the ass to deal with?

The Will—a brief mention

As I mentioned in the opener, the will controls who gets what. Your Final Letter should contain suggestions and advice. Do *not* make the Final Letter a set of instructions (especially instructions that contradict the will). Do you *want* there to be lawsuits?

Do you have a will? Half of Americans don't. There are some states that take half of any estate not controlled by a will—just to make up for the pain of having to deal with it. Having no will can potentially cost your heir one-half of everything they would have otherwise inherited. Or it could all go to the wrong heir.

Does your will address your intellectual property? If so, you are one of the rare few. Congratulations. If not, consider fixing this…now.

There are three (or four, depending on how you count them) major types of property:

- Personal Property – the stuff that you own (furniture, heirlooms, car, etc.)
- Real Property – the places that you own (land, house, condo, etc.)
- Business Property – which is mostly just a variation on the two themes above and isn't generally considered a type of its own
- Intellectual Property – creative works that you own (copyrights, trademarks, patents, etc.)

Your will should address all of these property types, with intellectual property being potentially the most valuable.

If you do have a will, how up-to-date is it?

- Was a kid born since your last update? (If so,

does your will include some statement like "all progeny" or does it list them by name so that your youngest will be left out because your will was written before their birth?)

- Was there a divorce? More than once, an old will has left the new wife and family destitute and given everything to the ex-spouse. Because you aren't around to ask, the court will typically adhere to your *written* instructions as the best indication of your intent.

- Is your will even still valid? Several years ago I moved from one state to another. My new state had much stricter requirements of what constituted a valid will. It was two years before I learned that my family would *not* be covered by my existing will from my former state of residence. I updated it fast.

There are many other considerations like these, which is why the will itself is the purview of lawyers and outside the scope of this book. If your estate includes IP, an estate tax plan should be created by a reliable lawyer specializing in intellectual property. Appropriately enough, they are called IP lawyers. Ideally, you want an IP lawyer who specializes in estate planning (yes, the laws are that squirrely).

The Inside Story: Allen Drury

Allen Drury wrote *Advise and Consent,* the 1960 *New York Times* #1 Best Seller of the Year. It was also the winner of the Pulitzer Prize (a dual feat not to be repeated until 2015 by *The Goldfinch* earned both accolades). There was even a major motion picture.

But five novels later, Mr. Drury was sick of New York publishing practices and left instructions in his will for the executors (his lawyer and the bartender at their favorite bar) to dismantle his literary estate upon his death, which they did very thoroughly. By 2013, it was the 27th most sought-after out-of-print title in America.

Also by 2013, Mr. Drury's heirs were living in poverty. After a 15-year struggle, they managed to regain control of *Advise and Consent* and its five sequels from the executors. Not understanding what they now had, they almost turned around and sold all rights to all six novels for $3,000 (which would have been a massive windfall for them at that time). A friend stopped them and the six titles are now back in print and partially supporting the heirs.

Lesson: You're dead, get over it. Once you're gone, it is up to your heirs to decide what to do with your legacy.

Intellectual Property (IP)

As mentioned before, IP is essentially all of the things *created* by a person. What these items are is only limited by the imagination because it is literally everything created by using the intellect (within certain rules and definitions of law). For the purposes of this book, I will primarily refer to books and works based on books, but that does not exclude IP in other fields, which may include: music, architectural designs, patented inventions, trademarks, choreography, and so much more.

See? That is one of the problems with IP: it has huge variety. Even in a seemingly narrow field such as a single book, there are potentially hundreds of rights to it, not merely print, electronic, and audio production. There are: limited editions, expanded editions, translations, graphic novels, films, plays, radio plays, merchandise…the list goes on and on. Audio production alone may then be subdivided into abridged, unabridged, dramatization, large-cast performance, inside the US, inside Senegal, in French, in French in Senegal… It boggles the imagination how many rights may be licensed individually. Ever see a *Game of Thrones* themed slot machine in Vegas? That's a tiny slice of George R. R. Martin's copyright.

This is all controlled by International Copyright Law (with some local variations that you need to find out for your own country). The name, at least, is actually less mysterious than it sounds: copyright is literally the right to copy something. Copyright Law, therefore, is the set of laws that control who gets to copy what, when. This can be a very complex area of the law, making lawyers who specialize in IP Law to be among the most expensive (sad but true, yet absolutely essential).

> *Dear Heir, What you need to understand isn't how to work with Copyright Law. What you need to understand is that Intellectual Property can be immensely valuable.*
>
> *Why is it so valuable? Not only can it be nearly infinitely subdivided, but it also has immense longevity. A house or condo ages. IP typically remains protected by Copyright Law in the US (and most places worldwide) for seventy years past the death of the author. Well-managed IP may not only support your children and grandchildren, but maybe even their children's children.*

Good Reading:

The Copyright Handbook by Stephen Fishman is perhaps one of the finest sleeping aids ever created, but it is also an *essential* education in copyright.

The Inside Story: Jane Austen

Jane Austen, often called the founder of the romance novel, is best known for her work *Pride and Prejudice*. She also wrote five other novels of varying popularity. She died in 1817 and by 1822 her heirs had allowed all of her novels to go out of print. For ten years they were unavailable.

In 1832, a savvy publisher purchased all of the copyrights outright for 250 British Pounds (that's just $26,000 in 2017 dollars). The original hardback sold for 18 shillings, about $96 today. So, for the price of 250 copies of Ms. Austen's books, her heirs sold all rights because they didn't understand what they had even though they had been involved in the original publishing process.

From 1832 to the present, these six titles have never been out of print and an 1813 second edition of *Pride and Prejudice* recently sold for $52,500—ironically, approximately twice what the heirs were paid for all rights to all six novels. The heirs never received another penny.

Lesson: IP can have long-term value that you can't anticipate and your heirs won't know that unless you tell them.

Keeping IP Fresh

We have already seen two examples of this in the Elvis Presley and Jane Austen estates. Once the people who understood business had control of the estates, they were able to "freshen" the IP and remarket it to new audiences.

There are many ways this can be done by a savvy estate manager.

Other examples include:

- Robert Jordan's estate hired Brandon Sanderson to complete the final volume of Jordan's massive Wheel of Time series after Jordan's death.

- I was a student projectionist for school films in the 1970s. We ran Saturday morning movies. I remember when suddenly the Elvis Presley movies were available for the first time since they were initially made. (They were a welcome break from the unending Jerry Lewis and Dean Martin slapstick comedies of that era.) That re-release created another economic boon for the Presley estate.

- Shortly after its re-release, Allen Drury's *Advise and Consent* was offered for a thriller promotional bundle I was preparing. I was thrilled to have first crack at this classic, even if only for the three weeks that promotion ran. In its first weeks back in print, my small promotion alone made the heirs approximately a third of what they'd been willing to sell all six novels for outright.

"But these estates are so large, how can they relate to me?" I can hear you asking.

First I will say that these estates grew so large and so valuable not by pure chance. There were good initial products, yes. But there was also good promotion of those products—often occurring after the creator's death. Consider this example:

The Inside Story: Lucia Berlin

In 2015, Lucia Berlin finally reached the *New York Times* Bestseller List with her short story collection, *A Manual for Cleaning Women.*

Prior to that, Ms. Berlin was a little-known author of short stories. She had some minor successes and received critical acclaim for her unique voice, but nothing spectacular.

A Manual for Cleaning Women out-sold all of her prior works—combined.

Oh, one other detail: she died eleven years earlier in 2004. It was her heirs who assembled and marketed this volume of her work so successfully. They made the IP fresh again, all without any new words from the author.

Lesson: Keeping IP fresh (and up-to-date with evolving technologies) may produce unexpected results for an estate of any size.

Bankruptcy—a quick note

As a holder of IP, you and your heir must be aware that you can't declare bankruptcy—ever. Why? Because the bankruptcy courts view IP as an asset of the estate. The court will seize these assets and sell them off to the highest bidder, often for cents on the dollar, and all of that potential future income will be lost and you'll never get it back.

The Inside Story: Mark Twain

Samuel Clemens, better known by his penname Mark Twain, was desperately close to bankruptcy. Only the last-minute advice of a friend protected his legacy.

Before declaring bankruptcy, Clemens transferred the rights to all of his IP over to his wife in order to protect it. (This trick no longer works: the courts have closed that loophole and can now reach back and frequently recover the IP assets that someone tried to give away at the last moment to protect them during bankruptcy. Even giving them away well before—if there's a possible implication that you knew you were headed toward bankruptcy—probably wouldn't protect them. And no, having the rights in a corporation in which you are an officer or significant stockholder doesn't typically protect those rights either.)

Lesson: It's a good thing that Clemens protected his Mark Twain IP—his estate was worth over $12 million (2017 dollars) at the time of his death.

Scams, Scams, and More Scams

There is perhaps no greater opportunity for scammers than authors. They don't even have to be deceased to be scammed.

Authors frequently see themselves strictly as

"artists," completely forgetting that they must also be business people. For those who actively state this ("Oh, I'm just an artist, I can't be bothered"), there is little excuse. But an heir is not a publishing professional. They're a student, engineer, school teacher, divorce lawyer, or car mechanic. Without a proper education in publishing, they are massive targets for scams.

Even more now than in the New York publishing-house era of domination (~1960-2011), the new world of independent publishing is throwing open the doors to future estate scammers.

I offer two sad examples below:

The Inside Story: Octavia Butler

Octavia Butler is often credited with being the greatest female science fiction author...ever! Her groundbreaking novels changed the very nature of how science fiction was written.

Now, just ten years after her death, her legacy is rapidly vanishing. Why? It was turned over to an estate manager. The manager is greedy or perhaps can't be bothered.

An editor attempted to license a Butler short story for inclusion in an anthology. The quote was very high. The editor argued and the price doubled. And again until the amount requested to reprint a single short story was more than a typical advance on a brand-new novel. Anything less than a major film offer is apparently treated with scorn.

This manager controls not only Ms. Butler's

estate, but dozens upon dozens of other literary estates, but I can't speak to how those are treated... or mistreated. One of the greatest science fiction writers of our era, male or female, is rapidly disappearing from the publishing landscape.

(Source: Introduction to *Women of Future's Past*, edited by Kristine Kathryn Rusch 2016)

Lesson: Be very careful who is managing your estate (we'll get into this in much more detail in Part II of this book).

The Inside Story: Patricia Cornwell

Patricia Cornwell, an immensely successful author of forensic medical thrillers, noticed a discrepancy in one of her bank accounts—on the order of $10 million.

Upon investigation, it turned out that a money manager she had hired embezzled over $50 million before being caught. Ms. Cornwell managed to recover the money, so it's not all bad news. However, in addition to the unimaginable stress and all of the legal work, I'm sure she managed to get very little writing done in the *five years* it took her to recover those funds.

Talking of this experience with Oprah, she stated that she wished she'd taken Oprah's advice from years before: "Always sign your own checks."

Lesson: You don't have to be dead to be scammed. Sign your own checks.

Good Reading:

Trial and Heirs by Mayoras and Mayoras

PART II: IMPORTANT TERMS

Okay, in Part I we laid the groundwork on this large and complex topic. In Part II we're going to explore certain aspects in more depth.

Now it is perhaps easier to see why your heir requires some level of guidance. The trick, I discovered, is to give guidance in a form that is useful to *them*. It should also be in a form that is useful to them, *for who they are.* The Final Letter to the nearby relative who has helped you on and off—or listened to your endless tales about the ups and downs of publishing—will be quite different from the one you write to your daughter, the medical doctor, who lives on the far side of the country.

Allow me to repeat that in bold:

Guidance *must be* in a form that is useful to the heir.

The Heir's Point of View (POV)

When you're writing a novel, especially early on, you worry a lot about the point of view of your character. To a writer, POV is which character's head you want to be in as you write a particular scene (hero, heroine, villain, sidekick, etc.). As you become more advanced, you realize that isn't the critical factor. (Non-fiction beginners have to figure it out much faster than fiction writers.)

In either fiction or non-fiction, one of the critical factors to captivating a reader is considering *their* POV—in this case: *the heirs*. An academic text is written very differently from this book, and the style of a Regency romance doesn't equate well to that of a hard-core thriller.

When writing the Final Letter to your heirs, you must consider *their* Point Of View very carefully. I even hesitate to use the shortening of POV for Point of View in this document as it is a term authors use far too lightly.

Your heir speaks English (or some other language). However, do they "speak" publishing? Even if they do, are they fluent in the language necessary to manage *your* IP? We'll revisit this concept several more times because it's so critical.

Some Vocabulary

Despite the need to communicate with the

heir in English (or other native tongue), there are some publishing terms that will make their lives significantly easier. There's no magic to these words, but as you'll see in the final chapter, I feel that it is important to include these definitions because there are important implications that are easier to explain with the correct language.

Property

Mentioned before, but the three types bear repeating:

- Personal Property – stuff you own, including bank accounts, investments, and retirement funds.
- Real Property – real estate, houses, condos, time-shares, private islands.
- Intellectual Property (IP) – stuff that you created that may be copyrighted, patented, or trademarked.

Who should own the IP?

(This is one of those moments where I remind you that I am not a lawyer nor do I play one on TV.) In my opinion, there is only one person who should hold IP, and that's the author, the author, or, did I mention, the author. But let's delve into that a little further.

Corporation

For an author, a corporation exists to control the legal tax burden.

That's it.

No, seriously!

A corporation does not protect an author from liability or claims of plagiarism or any of the other myriad lawsuits that may arise. Unless you have a massively complex estate, you are the owner or a significant owner of your corporation and are probably an officer of that corporation. Lawsuits pass through directly to you. Anyone who tells you that a corporation offers legal protection should be (in my opinion) backed away from—fast—perhaps while wielding a pointy stick.

A corporation is something that may be set up by a lawyer, but it is done upon the instructions of your accountant (hopefully an accountant who has experience with other writers or at least artists). For an author, corporations are all about the tax burden, not about liability.

If a corporation doesn't hold my copyright, then what does it hold?

I license my copyright *to* my corporation for the purposes of publication and promotion. This is where the lawyer comes in, making sure that employee vs. officer vs. owner vs. copyright owner don't become legally snarled together.

Again, like the will, this is outside the scope of this book.

Should the heir(s) be a shareholder of the corporation?

This may seem an obvious choice, however here are four reasons *not* to do that:

1. The heir becomes a drug addict or incurs a massive gambling debt. They use their rights as a shareholder of the corporation to give away their share to settle that debt. You are now legally in business with their supplier or bookie rather than your heir.
2. The heir marries, then divorces. But if they were married long enough, in certain states by a practice called Common Law, the ex-spouse now has a one-half share of everything the heir ever owned. Guess who you're in business with this time? And it goes on for the life of the author plus seventy years.
3. The multiple heirs don't get along. Death of a parent does not make warring siblings suddenly discover peace and cooperation. A successful or even a potentially wealthy estate isn't going to solve anything either. Attaching one or more of your heirs to the corporation as shareholders is only asking for difficulty, perhaps to the point where the estate becomes unmanageable while you are still alive.
4. A "dishonest" heir can use their power as a shareholder to disenfranchise you from your own estate.

"My heir(s) would never do that," you say on the last point? Guess again. The real-life examples are myriad.

But hold it, I'm an heir who received a corporation as part of the estate.

Dear Heir, Then you need to see how that particular corporation was set up. Ideally, there will be a master corporation book with at least once-yearly Board Meeting Minutes. The scope and intention of that corporation will be defined by the formation documents, bylaws, and (most importantly) any contracts. Some of those contracts may be between your new corporation and other corporations like publishers. But they may also include contracts that were between your new corporation and the author, making them now between the corporation and you, the heir.

Certified Public Accountants (CPA) and IP Lawyers

I've mentioned them a couple of times before. (If you live outside the United States, they are simply people who are legally certified to provide tax and legal advice on what can and can't be done with IP.) Unless you have an education in tax law, legally minimizing your tax burden is probably outside of your abilities. This book doesn't address that at all. However, I have listed a few titles in my suggested reading list at the end to help you get started on understanding how to work with a CPA.

Remember, not all CPAs and lawyers are created equal—someone graduated top of their class and someone at the bottom. An IP lawyer and a CPA with specific experience in working with artists and corporations are both absolutely required and very different from a divorce lawyer and a CPA who does your 1040 tax form each year. If you have a CPA, ask them if they actually do work with a writer's Intellectual Property.

Warning! There are dishonest CPAs. Even if they are doing the work honestly, they may say, "Sure, I understand how to work with writers and other artists," because they don't know enough about IP to know how unique it is. A CPA for a holder of IP has a very specialized knowledge set, just as an IP lawyer does.

How to find them? Ask a writer friend. Ask a successful writer. Ask a second CPA. Do not *assume,* as that can be a terribly expensive mistake. Or as another friend often says: trust but verify.

The Inside Story: Unnamed Author

An author, on the advice of their CPA, tried to run their publishing company worth nearly $10 million per year as a Schedule C business. (This is what is done with a small business on American IRS tax forms.) Because the author did this rather than forming a corporation, the IRS disallowed numerous deductions that are only available to corporations, not to individuals.

The author should have been able to deduct their writing retreat, transportation to and from that retreat, the vehicle they used for that, and a myriad other items. Because of bad advice from their CPA, the author has needlessly paid millions extra per year to the IRS and the IRS is now demanding that they pay millions more in interest and late fees.

I haven't used the author's name in this case, though it is a matter of public record, so that I can say the following: I hope that the author eventually sued that CPA for the massive scale of the malpractice in handling the author's accounting (in my non-professional opinion). A $10 million per year business should be a C-Corporation, perhaps multiple C-Corporations, not a "Schedule C" business documented on a 1040 form.

Had this been done properly, all of the deductions would have been allowed and the author's tax burden would have been lowered significantly even without careful planning of corporate structure. And why they didn't create a C-Corp after that first year mystifies me totally. The probably received *more* bad advice from the same CPA.

Lesson: When in doubt, get a second opinion.

Good Reading:

Tax Savvy for Small Businesses by Frederick W. Daily

Quick tip:

There are many on-line legal services that can make wills, set up trusts, and perform any of a number of tasks. These are stop-gap measures at best (any will is better than no will at all). However, a generic form with a few names plugged in may be legal, but it may also have gaps, holes, and irrelevant language that will cause future problems for your heirs.

Use them if you must, but get to a lawyer to at least review the document from these types of services as soon as you can. I have heard more than one story of a dishonest heir who walked through a loophole in one of these on-line service documents and disenfranchised all of the other heirs even though they were siblings or long-time business partners.

Contracts

A contract is a legal agreement that controls copyright.

Uh-huh.

Regrettably, this is both as simple as it sounds and as complex as can be.

Therefore, let's back up a little.

Copyright was earlier defined as "the right to copy." And I mentioned that those rights were wondrous (and potentially very profitable) in their variety.

A contract is what is used to control how each of those rights is licensed.

"I, the author, license to you, the magazine, the right to be the first party to publish my new short story, *An Amazon in London*. I promise I won't publish it anywhere else until three months after you do, and you'll pay me $300 for the use of that right."

The contract includes:

- Who = you and the magazine
- What = a license for the exclusive first publication right to the story
- In exchange for = a payment of $300
- For How Long = until 3 months after first publication

There are two very important points here, far more important than being paid: 1) a license of which specific bit of copyright and 2) when that right comes back to the author (which we'll address further in the very next section).

Copyright should never be *sold* unless you really, really, really know what you're doing—and even then it's probably a mistake. Besides the Jane Austen story I mentioned earlier, consider these two tales:

The Inside Story: George Lucas

George Lucas sold the Star Wars franchise

to Disney for just over $4 billion dollars (that's billion with a "B"). There's a winner, right?

Maybe.

While I'm sure Mr. Lucas knew what he was doing and had the very best advice money could buy (outside of Disney), I observe these two facts:

1. Disney's *The Force Awakens* grossed over $2B in its first month at the box office.
2. *Rogue One* grossed over $1B in its first month at the box office.

In their **first month!** I haven't seen any profit-and-loss statement (and never expect to), but that doesn't even include: action figures, video games, tie-in novels, soundtracks, any of that.

So, even in the most extreme case, copyright should almost never be sold, it should only be licensed. Now here's a crazy bit: in conversation, authors talk about "selling" copyright all the time, even though they mean "licensing." However, if a *contract* talks about the sale of copyright, watch out—it means it.

The Inside Story: Jack Ryan

Tom Clancy was unable to sell his first major novel to any publisher, so he sold *all* rights to his alma mater, Annapolis Naval Academy, for a paltry sum. Somehow a copy of the yet unpublished manuscript ended up in President Ronald Reagan's hands as he was descending from the Marine One helicopter onto the White House lawn.

The story goes that a reporter asked, "What are you reading?"

To which the President replied, "A novel called *The Hunt for Red October.* Best book I've ever read."

The book became a *huge* success. The movie that followed was a blockbuster success as well.

The problem? Tom Clancy had *sold* all of the rights to Annapolis. Out of pity, he was finally given a small "consulting fee" on the movie—the only money he ever made on that book or movie.

However, his problems didn't end there. Along with all of the rights, he had sold the rights to Jack Ryan, his main character. He had to purchase back the right to use Jack Ryan in future books.

Lesson: To authors or heirs reading this book, do *not* "sell" copyright. That is why IP lawyers negotiate contracts. Even then, tell them: license, not sell. Then check them on it. Twice.

Reversion of Rights

This is also a critical piece of knowledge for the heir. An heir probably shouldn't proceed with action based on anything in the following description, but they need to know what reversion is, as it has the potential to make them a lot of money in the future.

Dear Heir, go consult with a publishing professional or an IP lawyer if you need to actually do any of this.

Let's create two quick examples, a short story and the novel based on the story:

Top Quality Magazine

"I, the author, license my short story, *An Amazon in London,* to this magazine for first publication..." as referred to earlier.

Three months after publication, the rights revert back to me because that's the agreement in the contract. There may be another clause that says they can continue to reprint it in the magazine, but we won't worry about that here. The important right, the right for the author to publish elsewhere, has reverted to the author by contract.

Big Time Publisher

"I, the author, license the right to publish my novel, *The Amazon Who Took London by Storm,* (based on the short story) to a publisher." Or worse yet, I signed an agency agreement with a book agent.

At first glance it would appear that my book is tied up with that contract for the rest of my life plus seventy years. This isn't true for a number of reasons:

1. A well-written contract will have a "Reversion of Rights" clause just as the magazine did. It will be more complex, but it should be there. Then the rights will revert

(or can be reverted by request) whenever those stated conditions of time occur. Rather than time this could be a certain number of sales during a certain period of time or some other measure.

2. Let's say it's a really crappy clause or, worse yet, the author didn't make sure the clause was in there. Dead end, right? Nope. Rights were licensed for a fee, they can often be repurchased for a fee. There are ways to offer to buy back a publication license.

3. There are ways to legally break a contract if the other party (the publisher for example) is not performing their legal duties listed in the contract. (This almost definitely requires a lawyer, but it is possible.)

4. If all else fails, Copyright Law comes to our aid. There is a law that anticipates excited artists signing stupid and awful contracts. Or even a contract that may have been good in the beginning, but then a third company bought the publisher and the new company is now awful. Copyright Law states that you may request a "Reversion of Rights" after thirty-five years. This may not sound particularly impressive, but it is.

Let's go back to our example: I sold *The Amazon Who Took London by Storm* five years ago, I die peacefully in my sleep twenty-five years from now. The contract that I signed was crap and neither the publisher nor the agent will let go of the rights despite many attempts to get them back.

There *is* a way for the heir to revert the rights from that contract five years after my death, at thirty-five years after the contract itself was signed. In Year Thirty-five the heir would be able to republish that book themselves and make money for sixty-five more years (my life plus seventy years minus the five years the heir had to wait to force the reversion of the copyright). And there's *nothing* the publisher can do about it. (Once you miss thirty-five years, you're stuck.) The author can also exercise this return of rights if they are still living.

In other words: (Contract signing date) + (35 years) = (when all rights may be reclaimed— no matter what the contract said other than outright sale of the rights as mentioned above)

Quick tip:

The filing date comes several years before the thirty-five years from the date the contract was signed so check the law carefully and file early. Details are in Copyright Law and are explained in that fine reference *The Copyright Handbook*.

Dear Heir, It is important for you to know these possibilities exist. You can always hire someone who knows how to take advantage of these possibilities.

Contract vs. Terms of Service

There is a very important distinction here that seems complex, but really isn't.

A contract, as we've discussed extensively, is about licensing a slice of the total copyright (magazine publication, book publication in one country or worldwide, film, merchandise, etc.). It may be for a narrow purpose and a limited period of time (the ideal scenario) or it may be for a broad collection of rights until the end of copyright (death plus seventy years)—this all depends on the language in the contract that the author signed.

That said, it is the contract that controls the terms of this licensed bit of copyright with a publisher, filmmaker, toy producer, or whoever. A contract is most common where an *exclusive* use of a right is involved. Example: a book publisher licenses the exclusive right to publish your book both electronically and in print in the English language anywhere in the world.

Terms of Service (TOS) is also a legal, binding agreement, but more typically for a *non-exclusive* use of a right. For the author to publish a book themselves on Amazon, they are presented with a Terms of Service agreement. (It's that annoying thing where you have to click "I Accept these terms" before you're allowed to use a new piece of software.)

This too is a contract and should be read because it is legally binding. However, a TOS is not typically used for licensing copyright beyond a non-exclusive use, such as distribution for sale.

Amazon may be a poor example, because at the time of this writing they do handle some exclusive rights this way with their Kindle Select program. However, for the most part, Amazon, iBooks, Kobo, and most other book distribution (sales) sites are non-exclusive and are therefore using TOSs to handle these agreements.

The real distinction, and the reason all this is important?

A *contract* typically requires a Reversion of Rights by one of the mechanisms mentioned above before that exclusive right can be re-licensed elsewhere.

A *terms of service* agreement typically allows termination of the agreement at the click of a button.

The Inside Story: Terms of Service

There was a company that provided a TOS agreement for print distribution of an author's own book. For years the agreement included five separate documents that spanned over 120 pages of dense legalese. There were clauses that appeared to allow them the right to copy your book for free if they wanted to. In other words, if your book took off and became a huge success, they could sell *their own copy* of *your* book and never have to pay you a penny.

A friend actually hired an IP lawyer to review

this TOS and the lawyer was absolutely aghast and said that it would be better to starve than to ever sign this.

The agreement has since been changed; I've heard it's down to 60 pages…

Lesson: Always read any contract before you sign it, even if it is just some "standard" Terms of Service.

Need more proof? There was an online secure storage firm (one of the very first "save it in the cloud" services) whose original TOS allowed them to claim ownership of anything you uploaded to their storage site. That has since been changed after a storm of protest arose from those who actually thought to read what they were legally agreeing to.

Or? Most social media sites claim copyright ownership of anything placed on their site. If you publish your whole book on one of their sites? It's legally no longer exclusively yours. Load up your latest song? They can distribute it worldwide for free; and by the TOS that you accepted with that idle click when you were signing up, you legally granted them that permission.

Lesson Repeated: Always read any contract before you sign it, even if it is just some "standard" Terms of Service.

Trusts

This will be our last major piece of vocabulary.

A trust is a legal tool that lets you take a set of something, in our case IP, and place it all together so that it may be given, literally, *in trust* to an heir.

There are many ways to set up a trust (we're skirting the edges of my "not a lawyer" disclaimer here). However, I will say that a living revocable trust certainly looks very sensible to me. "Living revocable" means: set up while the author is alive and it can be revoked by the person who originally set it up (in other words, I continue to control my IP as long as I'm alive).

An irrevocable trust moves something permanently to someone else in ways that are *way* outside the scope of this book.

There are advantages to trusts. Here are my two favorite:

- A living trust will pass directly to the named beneficiary (heir) upon the trust holder's death. Then it doesn't get stuck in Probate Court (the court that takes care of wills and estates in the US). It simply moves to the named beneficiary. This means that a judge won't have to approve every choice the trustee makes. As the publishing of IP is an active business, it allows the heir to take immediate action to ensure that business, well, keeps doing business.
- Another big advantage is privacy. A trust moves from trustee to trustee and is therefore private. When a will moves through Probate Court, it becomes public record.

- Outside the scope of this book there are also:
  · Tax implications for future generations.
  · Charitable trusts to help minimize tax exposure
  · AB trusts that have to do with surviving spouse and other heirs.
  · And... Now you get why you need to talk to a lawyer about this.

Setting up a trust is a big-time consult with a lawyer. If your estate is small, it may not be worth setting up a trust because trusts cost money, may require additional tax filings, and more. How do you know how small is small? This will sound circular but it isn't: ask a lawyer. I'm sure Lucia Berlin's heirs simply inherited the rights to her seventy-seven short stories and three anthologies through her will rather than through a trust.

Do you need a will in addition to a trust? Yes. A trust moves to the trustee in a separate manner than the rest of your life which is most likely to be controlled by your will. What does *that* need to look like? At the risk of repeating myself, ask a lawyer.

Apparently the most common mistake in setting up a trust? Setting it up but not "funding" it. "Funding" is the process of legally moving the items, in this case IP, from your own possession into the trusts. In other words, failure to fund is going through all of additional expense and paperwork to set up a trust, but never transferring the actual copyright into it. Sounds obvious, guess not.

Good Reading:

Make Your Own Living Trust by Denis Clifford (Good information, but I still wouldn't do it myself. I used this reference so I had some understanding with which to talk to the lawyer.)

The Inside Story: the Power of Trust

(The following is a gross oversimplification of a very complex estate.)

A friend of mine married another friend—great news! They each had prior marriages, children, even stepchildren. She brought significant IP into the relationship and he brought a growing set of IP—both are writers, among a wide variety of other skills. He also brought a large block of fine-art IP from his deceased wife. He holds much of that for his dead wife's children but didn't want to mix that up with his new wife or her children. In addition, each of their literary estates also are split in various ways. (*I mentioned this was a complex estate.)*

Enter the trust. Through the intelligent use of wills and trusts, the new couple are each controlling precisely who receives what under a wide variety of circumstances (who pre-deceases, beneficiary disagreements, etc.). They were kind enough to share these with me and I'll simply say that it is impressive and, as far as I can tell, incredibly clean. Every point of contention that they could anticipate is clearly outlined in an overlapping set of documents that don't appear to have any contradictions between them.

Lesson: Even a very complex estate can be organized logically and legally using both trusts and wills—in consultation with a lawyer.

Quick tip:

Since I first talked to the couple mentioned above about the concept of The Final Letter, they have each drafted a complete letter similar to the one at the end of this book to assist their heirs in *managing* what the new couple is leaving to each different group of heirs in their wills and trusts.

Trustees

Picking your trustee, the person responsible for administering the trust, is almost as important as picking the heir. And, yes, the trustee can be the heirs, if they are competent and of an appropriate age.

However, will your heirs fight over how to manage the trust? Putting one heir in charge may not be a good choice either.

Will one of your heirs want to do all of the work? Perhaps one thinks a career of managing your legacy of IP sounds exciting—but you set up the other heirs as co-trustees who, it turns out, care more about sabotaging their sibling. Or maybe the other heirs *think* they know what's best but don't understand how unique managing IP can be?

This is a very important and tricky decision for you to consider carefully.

The Inside Story: The Lawyer

(A friend told me this story, but asked me to remove the names.)

My friend and his family received a large trust with the family lawyer acting as trustee. The long-term family lawyer died before the creator of the trust. No problem, the trust named the law firm in which the lawyer had been a partner as a secondary trustee.

The new lawyer who took control transferred the entire trust into his own name and then left the country.

The heirs were left holding nothing.

Lesson: Think long and hard about who manages your trust and any sole powers granted to them. Perhaps plan some form of signatory oversight by the heirs. Talk to an attorney, then talk to another. I make some suggestions on this in the next section.

The Inside Story: My Literary Trust

Right now I am in the process of reorganizing my own literary estate. Why? Because writing this book forced me to rethink things at a much deeper level. So, what follows is not advice, it is simply what I am in the middle of doing for my own estate as an illustration.

My initial will wrapped my IP into a trust upon my death. That trust then went to my heirs and they became the trustees. My line of heirs is very simple: wife, step-daughter, step-daughter's descendants (if/when she gets around to having some), sister, and finally a major charity. Each gets complete, individual control until they die. (Or are legally deemed incompetent. See? Another reason to have a lawyer in the loop: your estate planning should anticipate that possibility.)

I've already noted above the problems with this approach:

- My trust would be formed by the probate court. This increases the costs of probate significantly.
- Probate can easily take a minimum of a year. My heirs would have had to clear every action to maintain and enhance my publishing business through the court, inserting an awkward layer of management.
- My entire IP valuation (a fancy way of saying how much the court decides my IP is worth at the time of my death), is exposed to estate taxes. For example, while I think this is high: a court could decide that an estate that makes $50,000 per year will be worth that every year for the length of the copyright. My estate is suddenly worth $50,000 * 70 years =

$3,500,000 and would be taxed on that basis. As the laws (and tax rates in my country and state of residence presently stand), the heir could suddenly be facing a massive tax bill of over $180,000—far and above any actual income or funds on hand.

I am now in the process of creating a living trust (with the help of an IP lawyer who specializes in estate planning). We are expanding my personal estate plan (as defined by my will) into an estate tax plan (which will include the sensible use of trusts). I expect that the final structure will look something like the following:

- A living trust that includes my IP and the corporation I set up to manage that IP. The trust moves to the next named beneficiary at my death without traveling through probate court. (We'll talk about the various choices a trustee has on how to manage my estate in the very next section.)
- I will be the trust's trustee. That means that I still have complete control of my corporation and my IP for as long as I am alive and competent.
- Note: "Dynastic trusts" exist in very few states and mine is not one of them. I had originally thought/hoped (hence another reason why I needed a lawyer) that I could create a trust that was somehow magically outside of tax

law and each heir would merely inherit the trusteeship without a tax assessment...ever. Apparently it doesn't work that way (at least not in my state—I guess that Oregon pixie dust and tax law have very little influence on each other).

- IP Valuation is actually a rapidly changing area at this time (even more so than the e-publishing revolution of the first half of the 2010s). I've included this here mainly so that you don't have to panic the way I have been.

  · To be quite frank, the things I was reading about IP Valuation were scaring the crap out of me. How will the court estimate the total value of my estate for my life plus seventy years? What if my estate suddenly makes a killing in films? Or one of my series becomes the next *Game of Thrones* phenomenon ten years after my death? Or... If my estate was valued with all of those possibilities in mind, it was going to create a massive, gazillion-dollar tax assessment at my death.

  · It turns out that there are multiple ways to value an IP estate. Think of a house. There are at least three distinct values: the tax assessed value, the fair market value, and what you can actually sell the thing for. I had to sell a house in the middle of the recession: its tax value was around $350,000, its estimated fair market value was $450,000 (before the recession), and I priced it at

$350,000 then $300,000 and ultimately was able to sell it in a crisis sale for $205,000 two years later. (Let's just say that I didn't enjoy the recession of the late 2000s in the least.) And the massive movie example I gave above? That would be valuing my house based on the idea that one day it would be replaced by a huge resort hotel...not likely to happen or to be considered in probate.

· My IP follows a similar logic, creating drastically different valuations. It has a value if someone wanted to purchase it outright for the entire span of the copyright. It has a fair market value of perhaps the current annual income of the estate at my death times seventy years or some similar calculation. And it has an actual value upon my death that might assume a rapid fall off in value over five years, down to some much lower base income that tapers slowly toward nothing over the final sixty-five years. (This is assuming no marketing wizard, like Priscilla Presley in the story mentioned in the first chapter, or TV series steps in to increase its long-term value.)

• Once my trust is established, I will then be revisiting my estate tax plan and trust with the lawyer approximately every five years, or whenever I go through a major change, to keep it up to date. It could be a change in the beneficiary plan, or in response to a significant revision of estate tax law. What if I become massively successful? I can expand from a single trust into a set of trusts that might include a charitable trust, which also serves to keep my estate tax burden as low as possible.

- A trust is about protecting my IP by transferring it in the most accessible form to the beneficiary (heir) *and* minimizing the tax burden for that heir at the same time.

- I believe my heirs to be sensible folks. Therefore, rather than naming an outside trustee and perhaps giving my heirs some form of oversight and control, the line of my own trust's beneficiaries is identical to my will's line of heirs.

Quick Tip:

Your decisions must be based on your own needs and wishes, not my example above.

I recently spoke with a woman who is setting up her will to liquidate all of her assets on her death, and bequeath those funds and her IP to a charity because she doesn't want anything to go to her potential heirs—a highly contentious group of siblings and an ex-husband. Every situation is unique. You must consider your own very carefully.

PART III: Managing the IP

Whether you are the author writing your Final Letter or the heir who didn't receive one, *managing* the Intellectual Property is the single most difficult task you face. This section is the result of my efforts to clarify these choices for both my heirs and for several groups of professional writers to whom I've presented this topic.

The heir has a number of ways they can choose to manage the Intellectual Property they have just received directly or through a trust. These options closely mirror the author's own choices. If the heir is not the trustee, these options still apply. There are a lot of variations that are possible, but I think that they are just that, variations of what I have listed below.

I've come up with a list of six options, of which I personally feel five are viable and one is a warning. As we move down through this list, the amount of effort required by the heir decreases, but so does the amount of money they are likely to earn. However, the heir managing an IP estate directly, but poorly, may make less money than if they paid the right person to do it correctly. The amount of control the heir can exercise decreases with each step as well.

Here's the list (then we'll get into the details):

1. Manage it themselves
2. Hire fee-based services
3. Hire a publisher (full- or part-time depending on the size of the estate)
4. Hire a share-based manager
5. Give it away
6. Sell it outright

1. Manage the Estate Themselves

Let me first say that I can barely do this myself. Unless your heir is deeply involved in the modern world of publishing and marketing—and is willing to keep up on innovations in the industry—this probably is not a viable option.

They have to love it.

Think Priscilla Presley and the Elvis estate (though I expect she was more motivated by love of her daughter than worried about her ex-husband's legacy).

2. Hire a Fee-based Service

There are companies that will format and upload a book for a fixed fee. Or run a social media marketing campaign for a fixed fee.

Your heir can choose to keep a significant portion of the profits by using this method. The heir chooses what needs to be done with what titles, but can subcontract any of the work that they aren't comfortable doing.

I do this myself right now. I subcontract my cover designs and my final proofreading. I have an assistant (who also happens to be my spouse) who is paid for research, copyediting, laying out titles for print formatting, uploading titles to various sites for sale, and other tasks. I do this not because I can't do most of these tasks (though I'm a seriously crappy proofreader and only a marginal copyeditor), but rather if I do them all, I won't spend any time writing.

This solution leaves the heir in complete control of every step. This is both an advantage and a disadvantage. With more control comes more responsibility and the need for more knowledge and time.

3. Hire a Full- or Part-time Publisher

For very successful authors, this may already be in place: a person who is hired to be in charge of most aspects of publishing and marketing. In these cases, the author (and eventually the heir) is only responsible for reviewing the plans put forth by the publisher. The level of involvement by the heir (greater or lesser control of how the IP is managed by the publisher) will be up to the heir and how they instruct the publisher.

For smaller estates, I think we will see a surge of this type of service. A service that offers all of the capabilities of a publisher, but is working under the general direction of the author or heir—typically through a series of weekly or monthly meetings. (Courtesy of modern technology, this person or service does not need to be local.)

How are they paid? That's the important part.

Rather than being paid by the task as a fee-based service would be, they are paid as an employee. That payment can be an hourly wage for so many hours per month. Or it could also be for a base salary plus a commission. Consider the idea of offering them a lower salary and a percentage of any profits. The better they do at their job, the more they get paid.

4. Hire a Share-based Manager for the Estate

If you don't already know my opinion, I'll restate it once more: *Don't Do This!*

Note that in the second and third options

above, the fee-based service or employee works for you and may be hired or fired at will. A share-based manager takes a percentage of all income, usually contractually and often for the length of the copyright (author's life plus seventy years).

This is how an agent works. For 15% of all your writing income (or sometimes more), they will agree to do whatever they're in the mood to do. If it is too unimportant, as the manager for Octavia Butler's estate apparently feels, then they won't do anything. Their 15% loss equals your 85% loss, but it is completely out of your control for as long as whatever contract was signed with them is valid.

Did I mention my opinion? *Don't Do This!*

5. Give It Away

This actually isn't as ludicrous an option as it sounds. Many charities and some universities and colleges are set up to receive and manage an estate made up of Intellectual Property.

A few personal thoughts on this (again, not legal advice).

1. Nothing says that you have to give them 100% of the estate's profits. Consider offering them 50% of the profits (or some other negotiated amount). If they do their job well, they will make 50% and you will make 50%. Your only required effort will be to deposit the check.

2. Perhaps give them the rights to manage the

IP without giving them the IP itself. Then, if they aren't performing well after a pre-agreed length of time (perhaps three years), you still hold the IP and can take it back and go hunting for another, more pro-active charity.

3. This is one of the places where a trust is a very useful concept. You give the charity the right to manage the trust, but you retain the ownership of the trust.

4. *Don't try to do any of this without a lawyer.*

6. Sell It Outright

Again, just as George Lucas did with Star Wars, the copyright can be sold outright for a one-time fee that you feel is worthwhile. It must be a fee that you will be comfortable with no matter how much money the new owner figures out how to make with it. I suspect this is what Mr. Lucas actually did: sold Star Wars for enough money that he could do any project he wanted to in the future without worrying about financing.

There are many possible variations on these six options, but I think this provides the basic guidelines to each option that might be considered.

Do each of these sound like gross over-simplifications? Absolutely. Hiring a service or an employee requires clear definitions of work, roles, payment, employment, etc.

Can an accountant be hired to manage

the money? Sure, though considering Patricia Cornwell's experience, I would have the accountant write out the checks, but have yours be the only valid signature.

Can a full-time marketing person be hired as well as a publisher? Absolutely, if the estate is big enough to justify it. I know several writers with seven to ten full-time employees to run their publishing company—under the author's direction.

You, and your eventual heir, will have to think about what fits each of you and your estate best.

Now you can start to see why I'm not trying to give any specific advice. The answers will be different for everybody. At my present scale of success, I am just now transitioning out of option #1 (doing it all myself) and into option #2 (paying for services as I need them). Also at my present scale, my heirs have indicated that they would jump straight to option #3 (hiring a part-time publisher) and go for minimal involvement with that publisher except for checking on profitability and signing all of the major checks themselves. Your solution needs to fit you.

PART IV: Where's the Money?

There are two questions that an estate lawyer will ask first when approached about an estate. (Possibly even before asking if you're feeling okay.)

- Is there a will?
- Where's the money?

And they might ask them in the other order.

This isn't as crass as it sounds. If an heir doesn't know where the money is, that tells the lawyer a great deal about the amount of work that is going to be required to organize the estate. If the heir knows where the money is, the next question will be:

- How much money?

This will then tell the lawyer the scale of the estate. A massive estate will take far more effort than a small one and this question is the easiest measure.

Personal Money vs. Publishing Money

Personal money is often very confusing for an estate, but even so, it is much simpler than IP money. Here's why.

Personal money is either in bank accounts or investments (stocks, IRAs, 401Ks, CDs, real estate, etc.). How easy it is to track all of these down will depend on how good the deceased was at organizing their records. I know one heir who was uncovering new investments for years, mostly by the notices from the multitude of banks the deceased relative had used, regarding whatever unknown CD was now up for renewal. That had been their safety plan, investment CDs at as many different banks as he could find in his city. Too bad he was so poor at keeping records.

Today's personal money may also be in PayPal or any of a number of other services, but most of these behave just like bank accounts. Direct income (like paychecks) stop when the person stops working, though pensions may keep paying.

Money tied up in publishing never sits still. As an example of its complexity, I made a partial list of how my own publishing money will continue moving—even after my death.

In-bound Money (Income)
- From distributors: Amazon, iBooks, Kobo, and several others.

- From contracts with my book publisher. Even if I am no longer creating new books for this publisher, books I have previously published with them remain under contract with that publisher until the rights are reverted. The contract survives my death.

- From contracts with an agent—often an author isn't paid by the publisher but rather by their agent (I don't have one). An agent, and any contracts, with them must be tracked just as clearly as a publisher and your publishing contracts. Actually, I highly recommend that the author send notice to your agent and publisher and arrange for the publisher to split the payments (typically 85% to the author and 15% to the agent) and pay the author directly. Not only does this expedite payment and avoid any number of potential agent issues, but it also simplifies the paths the money travels for the heirs.

- From contracts I have made with various magazines and anthologies. Some of these are one-time publications, but some include extra payments if the anthology is ever made into an audio book, etc.

- Oh, did I mention the two cooperative projects I have set up with other authors who will be paying me?

- I also receive monthly payments from direct sales from my website.

- Sporadic income arrives from book bundling sites where a book or short story is sold in conjunction with others.
- Online lectures that I have set up that don't require me to do any more work once I create them, yet continue to sell.
- I hope to someday have film options or movie royalties.
- The more successful I am, the more paths the money comes from: different publishers, different countries, and different contracts and agreements.

Quick tip:

Remember, it is up to you to keep everyone notified of changes to address and accounts. If you close a bank account, you may be shutting down a line of direct deposit unless you notify the vendor/publisher of the change.

Out-bound Money (Expenses)

- Automatic bank account withdrawals for website hosting, subscriptions to services, and other online tools.
- Automatic withdrawals for on-going and scheduled advertising campaigns.
- If I have staff? Payments and payroll expenses that are due to them.
- Book and cover designers.
- Insurance.
- Lawyers.

- Accountants.
- Perhaps translators for foreign language editions.
- Voice talent and engineers for audio editions.
- Money I owe to other authors for cooperative projects I am responsible for.
- The more successful I am, also the more ways that money is moving out.

Neither of these, income or expenses, stop moving simply because I did something as trivial as die.

Why is this so complicated? Because publishing is a business with a life and responsibilities of its own. Whether I have two titles or two hundred, it's still a business. Organizing your money into an understandable form for the heir is perhaps one of the greatest gifts you can give them. You'll see how I do this in my sample Final Letter at the end of this book. But even creating a simple list for your heir similar to the one above, but with actual names of each of those avenues of cash flow, would be a great help.

How to Get to the Money

This is also a necessary step. Typically a death certificate and a copy of the will are enough to get access to bank accounts. However, how do you access an online account like PayPal? Or a distributor like Amazon? Or an expense like a website host?

Today's world is all about passwords. Using the same password everywhere is an invitation to get everything hacked at once. So we use multiple passwords. Where are those kept safe?

Passwords in your head are of no use to any heir. "Well, they can just use my email account to reset any passwords they need to." Makes sense. Except how many email accounts do you have, and what are *those* passwords? (I won't even mention that most email accounts legally cease to exist at the time of your death, even if practically they may continue on for a time. In other words, your heir may not be able to get to your e-mail account to reset your passwords. Read those pesky Terms of Service.)

"I have a list of my passwords." Fine. Does the heir know where?

"I use a password tool." Dashlane is one of the popular password managers at the time of this writing. And how do you access your password manager? With a password?

I could go on and on, but I think you get the point. You must find a consistent and complete way to pass on your passwords to your heir that is within your level of comfort about the security of doing so. (Don't really trust your heir? Don't give them your passwords while you're still alive—don't give them the chance to prove your concern valid. I've heard of more than one estate that was "stolen" by the heir because they were tired of waiting for the author to die.)

Personally, I worked in IT for almost thirty years and I know just how vulnerable computer systems are, even in this day and age. Mine are written down, with one key piece missing. My heirs have been verbally informed as to what that key piece is. If someone steals the list without that piece, it's useless. This matches *my* personal level of paranoia about password security.

Late Breaking News

As this book was going to press, one of the biggest password services was hacked. Their notice to customers? "Customer data was compromised, including the ability to decrypt encrypted data."

My personal level of surprise? None.

The Inside Story: The Lost PayPal Account

I have a friend who was named executor for his best friend's estate. Regrettably, his best friend was far from organized. Through a lot of detective work, my friend was eventually able to uncover and unlock a dozen bank accounts and a PayPal account.

And then he discovered a second PayPal account.

The deceased did a great deal of business online, as the first PayPal account had shown. The problem with the second account was that not only was the password lost but the email account for resetting the password had long since been closed down and couldn't be reinstated. PayPal did what they could to assist, but after hundreds of attempts and dozens of hours of work, the account was as locked as ever. Whatever money is in that account, or is flowing into that account from who knows where, still remains lost years later. (Perhaps the funds will be recoverable when they are moved into the state's unclaimed property division. If you don't know about this, visit: www.unclaimed.org.)

Lesson: For my own level of electronic paranoia, I write a list with all of my accounts and passwords. If you don't trust your heir with your that list, give them to the executor or the lawyer who holds your will in a sealed envelope. Or place them in a safety deposit box (and make sure to tell your heir that there *is* a safety deposit box). And keep the list updated.

Tracking the Money

As a creator and seller of Intellectual Property, you are running a business—be it small or enormous.

Initially, when the business is truly small, it can be run from a checkbook. Even a simple, handwritten ledger is a good idea from the very beginning.

As your business grows, moving to an electronic

system such as Quicken, QuickBooks, or Sage 50 (formerly Peachtree) is highly recommended. First, these programs have great organizational and reporting tools. But more importantly, they track, over time, all of your income and expenses. This will give your heir a simple-to-access view of your business. Even if all they do is hand the information over to an accountant, it will vastly simplify unraveling your estate and your business.

I have a friend who runs a half-million-dollar business from his corporate checkbook. He makes my head hurt. By the time my business had grown past $1,000 per year, it was in Quicken. By the time it crossed $20,000 per year, it was in QuickBooks.

Make the money easy for your heir to find, even if you don't make it easy for them to access yet.

PART V: Organizing It All

I imagine that at this point you are feeling completely overwhelmed.

- Passwords
- Money
- Vocabulary
- Different ways to manage IP
- Trying to remember what IP *is*
- CPAs
- Lawyers
- Trusts
- Copyright Law
- ***How do I communicate all this to my heir?!?***

Step One in communicating your estate to your heir: ***Be Organized.***

Let me start with a story. Several years ago, I wanted to rework the cover of a short story I had published a few years earlier. That should be easy because the short story was filed here…no, there? Under that folder? Inside that directory? Even search tools didn't help.

I finally found the short story, but more by chance than planning. It was because I had conceived of the story as having one title, but changed it at the last minute and left it under the old title in a folder filled with other bits and pieces. So I finally had the file and the title, but the cover was still nowhere to be found. Was it in a "novel covers" folder mixed up with…

You get the idea.

This started me thinking about file organization. And when I started working on *this* book, I realized that there was much more that I had to organize if my heir wanted any chance of understanding what I had left.

As we'll see in the next section, some of this organization is inherent in the "Final Letter." But some of it isn't so simple.

The Book Files

By the time I reached thirty novels, twenty short stories, a couple of collections, and a kajillion new ideas, my book files were in absolute mayhem. As the author, I was spending time, even significant time as described above, locating files.

It was well past time to organize everything. You can use any system that makes sense to you, and hopefully your heirs as well. As one example, here's the organization that worked for me on my computer. (Each bullet point below is a separate folder.)

- Books – contains all of my books
- Series name (sub-folder of Books)
  - Book title – I often number it by the order of the book in the series (*DF1-Target Engaged* for the first book in my Delta Force romance series). My active working files for the book itself are here.
    - Cover – this will have all of the final versions of my covers (the ones I need at different resolutions).
      - Working – where I store the working documents for that cover.
    - Ref & Archive – all of my research and reference notes as well as my old versions.
    - I also have one other file that I store in the Books folder. I have a list (mine happens to be in Excel) of my characters. I accidentally named a villain in my foodie thriller series and the hero of my military romance series with the same name. Then I had a fan say they couldn't wait to see the story of how I was going to morph my villain in one series into the hero in another. (I went back and changed the villain's name). My wife (bless her) then went back and reread all of my books and made a list of every single name. I also track a few other

items in this file: hair, eyes, rank, height, and nicknames. For my purposes, that is sufficient. For me this is a critical file. Even if no heir will ever care about it, I thought it was worth mentioning.

- Short Stories
  - · This will have the exact same structure as Books.
- Audio
  - · Because these are such unique projects and not necessarily associated with every book, I have chosen to store these in a separate folder. Each, again, follows my master structure, making my life and my heir's life easier.
- Business – This is a critical folder, perhaps even more important that the IP folders. This one folder contains everything necessary to know about my business.
  - · Accounting Programs Data
  - · Contracts
  - · Corporation
    - - Formation documents
    - - Meeting minutes
  - · CPA – for all communications back and forth.
  - · Estate Planning – this includes copies of my will and the most recent Final Letter.
  - · Taxes – any electronic tax forms I've received or sent.
  - · The Master Password *file* (we've already

discussed this in the prior section and this is where I store mine).

· The Publishing the Book *file* (more on that file in a moment).

- Marketing
  · This is a folder rapidly spiraling out of control for me. Do I organize it like the folders above (what marketing I've done for each title)? Or is it better if I organize it by the Market (here are all of the Facebook ads, there are the Bookbub ads)? Or…
  · I think the key is that these are not actual IP folders (except for perhaps drafts of ad copy). Their organization isn't essential for the heir. Helpful, but not essential.
  · I do have a few dedicated folders here:
    - Marketing research studies
    - Social media graphics
    - Website graphics
    - Blog tours (by title) for books that have received blog tours.
- Other Writing
  · This folder contains all the miscellaneous crap. Ideas I started but never finished. Presentations I've given. Class notes I've taken. All that noise that I refer to but no one except some crazed academic could ever possibly care about. By storing it all here, I keep it out of my way and out of my heir's way.

Quick Tip:

To display these folders in the order I want them, I add a letter to their name: A-Books, A-Short Stories, B-Accounting, B-Business, C-Marketing, D-Other Writing, etc.

Summing It Up

This all sounds like a nightmare to do, doesn't it? It's not really, I was pleased to find out. Once I had planned out a folder structure I was happy with, it only took a long afternoon to get everything properly filed away.

One thing that I never found? That short story cover—it had gotten deleted somewhere along the way. Now that everything is filed properly, I rarely lose anything and I'm able to locate it quickly.

Here's an example of what one part of my structure looks like (a screen shot from my computer):

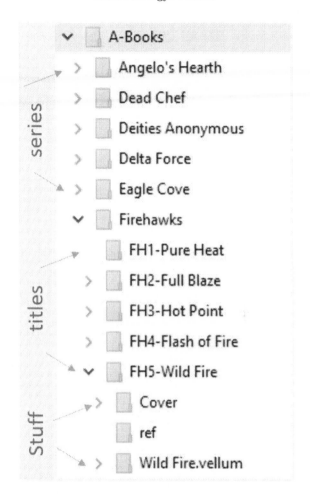

Publishing The Book—*The* Master File

This is the single most critical file for the heir, at least as important as The Final Letter and far beyond any mere IP file. This is the file that tracks every single published title and all of the critical aspects of that publication.

How in the world can so much information be packed into a single file? I'm so glad you asked. Because once it is done, it is very simple for the heir (or the publisher hired by the heir) to understand the status of your business. For that matter, there is no way I could run my business without this file. Even if you're lazy about backing up other files, back this one up *at least* weekly. If the apocalypse comes and you're sprinting for the hill?

Grab this file on your way out the door.

The Structure of the File

This file is most easily maintained in Excel (or other spreadsheet software). One of the reasons I recommend a spreadsheet rather than a database is that for every person who knows how to operate a database, there are ten thousand who know how to use a spreadsheet.

My secret is that every title has one *and only one* line in this spreadsheet. All of the most essential information is therefore easily readable in that line.

Dear Heir, Unless you intend to be involved in the day-to-day operation of this business you don't care about the contents of this file. What you do care about is getting it into the hands of the person handling future publication and marketing for you. If the author didn't create some version of this file for you, I give you permission to cuss them out soundly.

Let's look at what my version of that file includes:

- The Basics
  - Title
  - Genre
  - Series
  - Serial # in that series (ie. Book #4)
  - Independently or traditionally published (which will imply whether or not a contract needs to be tracked down)
  - # of words
- Production
  - # of pages if there's a print version
  - Price of e-book
  - Price of print book
  - Price of audio book
  - Print ISBN
  - Is this a Bowker or a 3rd party ISBN (The heir doesn't need to worry about what this means. However, if the publisher you're interviewing can't explain it to you, look

for another candidate. Bowker is the US distributor of that 13-digit number in the barcode on the back of a printed book.)

- Publication Dates
  - Initial Publication Date
  - If traditionally published: the rule for reversion of rights
  - If traditionally published: the date at which the 35-year copyright reversion rule may be used. You must file prior to the 35th year. Look up the details and perhaps add a column for that as well.
  - If independently published: a column for when the title was published to each distributor (Amazon, iBooks, Kobo, etc.). I will change this date if I upload a revised version to that channel, but I won't change the Initial Publication Date.
- Other Dates
  - Audio release
  - Audio reversion of rights rule
  - Date uploaded to: (any reminders I need to make sure I do something)
    - Website
    - Newsletter
    - Patreon
    - YouTube
    - Etc.
  - Filed Copyright with your country's Copyright Office

Below is an example of my Publishing the Book master file. It includes two titles: the first independently published, the second traditionally published. (I have shown these as separate pieces strictly for visibility. In actuality, this is long lines, one per title.) These fields do not exactly match my list above which is fine (I wanted to show that you need to make the file fit your way of doing business).

THE BASICS

Main Series	Sub Series	Series #	Title	Novel, SS,Coll	Genre	Publisher	0.1M Words	Print Pages
MM		1	My Amazing Title	N		Me	45,000	242
MM	SS	1	My Cool Short Story Title	SS		F&SF	4,000	65
MM	SS	2	My Cool Short Story Title	SS		Asimovs	4,800	72
AS		1	My Other Cool Title	N		BigPub	85,000	346

PRODUCTION				
PRICING				My
e-book	print	audio	Print-ISBN 13	ISBN
$ 4.99	$7.99	$ 9.99	0123456789012	Y
$ 2.99	$5.99			

MASTER DATES					
Pub Date Initial	Revert Rules	copy right	35 year Revert	File to Revert	
1/1/01					
	90 days				
	120 days				
	500/yr				

INDIE PUBLICATION DATES

Amz	Apple	B&N	Kobo	D2D	Google Play	Create Space	In...

MORE DATES

Audio	Web site	Mailing List	Good reads	Patreon	Other A	Other B

Quick tip:

Do you hate Excel or vice versa? Well, I created a blank starter file for you. Simply go to the following URL and click on the link to download. (You could also do this in Word, think one page per title, 1 line per item. For example: Title: Your Title, Series:…)

http://www.mlbuchman.com/mybooks/

Whoever takes over my publishing business will love me for this file, but frankly, I'm the one who gets immense utility out of it. I can see the status of every title at a glance, even the pre-release ones.

Where ARE the files?

This may seem obvious to you, you use them every day. Perhaps not so much to your heir. Are they:

- On your laptop
- On your desktop (or worse, a bit of both)
- On a server in your house
- In the Internet Cloud somewhere, if so, where: Google, Microsoft, Adobe Creative, Amazon Simple Storage Service, Amazon Glacier, Dropbox… (I won't ask what happens if one goes out of business or suffers a catastrophic failure.)

Another issue is the format of the files. My

sister is one of the nation's leading digital archivists and a frequent speaker on the topic. Her job is to make sure that anything she photographs to preserve (which has included a Gutenberg Bible and Napoleon's actual map of the Battle of Waterloo complete with his markings as he tracked the battle), will always be accessible. She frequently gets upset with me on this point: Are chunks of my IP tied up in old file types in old formats that are proprietary to one particular company? For posterity, hers can't be. Yours and mine shouldn't be.

The Inside Story: a Lineage of Mac-ness

I have an author friend with six Macintoshes of varying age. Going back for a short story, he'll take an old disk, plug it into Mac #2 (which was his main machine when he wrote that story), upgrade that file to Mac #3's file format, then from there he can jump to a different disk format using Mac #4... When I confront him on the marginal reliability (and long-term pain-in-the-backside nature) of this process, he points to his paper-filled filing cabinets and says, "They're all there anyway."

He and I agree that's a scary statement from someone who lost his first two novels and a large number of short stories and poems to a house fire early in his career. I understand the logistics of the problem faced by a prolific writer with forty years of IP.

Lesson: The real question isn't how he is solving it—the real question is how *you* will solve it for *your* heirs?

———————————————

Think about your IP. Are significant chunks of it locked up in WordStar, Samna, or XyWrite (especially popular with journalists)? Are those files backed-up off site?

Perhaps all of your IP is in current formats. Mine was too—when I started writing twenty-five years ago—in a program so popular that I *knew* it would never go away: WordPerfect 5.1 for DOS. Now I bless the long and painful couple days where I took all of those files and saved them into an open format like RTF.

Consider how technology has changed in the last quarter century. I hope to still be writing a quarter of a century from now and I hope my heirs will be making money from my IP for an additional *three-quarters* of a century after I die. Writing is a long-term business…remember to take the long view when considering how to archive your work.

The Paper Files of Business

There are numerous paper files that come with a publishing business. I recommend placing them in folders in a file drawer, file cabinet, or set of file cabinets depending on the size of your business.

Tell your heir, "That's where the paper files are." Feel free to kick the file cabinet in disgust, even though it isn't the cabinet's fault.

My paper files look something like this:

- Current Year
  - Federal taxes
  - State taxes
  - City taxes
  - Payroll (if any)
  - Bank statements
  - Receipts
  - (Once a year these are all bundled together and then stored for seven years)
- Lifetime
  - Book contracts
  - Short story contracts
  - Tax returns as filed
- On the shelf
  - A printed copy of every single story I've written or had published. That way, if all else fails, the heir can have that paper copy scanned or re-typed and your IP isn't lost.

Simple and straightforward...unless they're scattered about, some in this stack and some more over there...

You're a business, behave like one.

Dear Heir, They didn't do this? My best suggestion is to start a file box and place each item you find into the appropriate

folder (the list above are the critical ones).
What words of frustration you offer up in
the name of the deceased during this painful
process I leave entirely up to you.

PART VI: The Final Letter

Below you'll find a generic copy of the Final Letter that I wrote to my heirs. After all of the discussion above, it should look very familiar. I didn't include an electronic copy of this document with my book for a specific reason: I feel that it should be in your voice to your heirs. However, if you want to use this word for word, you have my permission to do so. If it gets the job done? *Please* do so.

At the very end I'll talk about putting together the "Final Package"…which is mostly this letter and a few of the files mentioned here.

Contents

- Introduction
- Where can I find the key stuff?
- Will, trust, bank books
- Some helpful vocabulary
- Basic publishing education
- Where's the money?
- Where can I find everything else?
- All the publishing crap
- Master file explanations

Do you notice anything different about this list?

IT'S IN ENGLISH!

FRIENDLY ENGLISH!

I mentioned that I'd be coming back to this point: remember the heir's Point of View when you are writing your Final Letter. You've died, the estate is in whatever terrifying state it's in, and the heir's head is spinning. Make it friendly and easy for them, and there's a chance that your legacy will live on.

Quick tip:

I treat it just like a letter. I write it in first person to my heirs.

Okay, here we go:

THE FINAL LETTER

ESTATE PLANNING -READ ME
Rev date: 03/09/2017 (you really want this)

WHERE TO START

INTRODUCTION

This document is intended to be a guide to where all of the pieces can be found. Any suggestions on how to manage the estate are just that, suggestions. They are the best ideas I have at the writing of this document on how to maximize the value of the estate.

This is intended to be a "live" document. Two to four times a year a revision of this document and other "key" files as described below will be sent to all possible executors.

This document is intended to be strictly informational. Anything that conflicts with the Will or Trust documents is a mistake. The Will and Trust documents control, not this.

WILL AND TRUST

There are copies:
- In the fire safe or safety deposit box.
- Filed with the [*named*] law firm.
  - · [*Their contact info*]
- PDF in this directory-though I'm not sure if that is a legally valid copy, but it is a scan of the executed original.

The will's and trust's intent, in plain(ish) English:
- If I was too much of a doofus to put all of my IP (Intellectual Property) into a trust, it will pass on to my heir(s) as directed by the will. If I did set up a living trust, it will move directly to the heir based on the trust's beneficiary setup.
- That trust goes to [*my spouse*].
- If she's gone, it goes to [*my kid/kids*].
- If *kid/kids is/are* gone...
- Failing all that, it goes to [my old college] to benefit the Writing Department.

Note: *I have already approached my college to be sure they are comfortable with this. At this writing, that is unclear, but we're working on it.*

More on various ways of "Managing the Trust" below.

WHAT THE HECK IS ALL THIS ANYWAY?

A FEW KEY VOCABULARY WORDS

Which will make the rest of this easier:

- **Intellectual Property (IP)** – There are 3 key types of property:
  - Personal property – all the *stuff.* Belongings, bank accounts, retirement funds, cars, private jets (wouldn't that be sweet?), etc.
  - Real property – Real estate: land, house, condo, Tahitian hut on the beach, etc.
  - Intellectual Property – All the stuff I wrote. The actual words. This document is all about this type of property.
  - Some of this property may belong to the Corporation. For example, the corporation owns the computers and printers, but not much else at this time. The main thing they own is a license to use and manage my copyright, see *My Corporation, Inc.* below.

- **IP Lawyer** – this is a specialist in IP law, quite different from your typical family lawyer or estate lawyer. Absolutely essential when dealing with any major contract.
- **CPA** – Certified Public Accountant. These come in a wide variety of shapes and sizes. One used to dealing with artists' corporations is the best choice. If whatever CPA mentioned below is no longer functioning or considered to be desirable, a good CPA can be found by asking friends, especially friends who are successful writers, actors, directors, playwrights, or other creators of IP.
- **Copyright** – Literally the right to copy. Once I've written something, I can then exercise (use) my copyright or I can license it for others to use. *NEVER* sell it. Here are a few of the many ways it can be exercised or licensed. You don't need to understand these at this point, just understand that there are lots of ways to make money with my IP, including:
  - Print & e-book often done together as Publication Rights, for example to a traditional book publisher. (Amazon and those sorts of things are different and discussed below under Distributors.)
  - First publication rights (which means they only get to publish it first, then after a contracted amount of time, the rights come back). This is how magazines and anthologies typically license rights.

- · Movies (big screen or TV)
- · Plays (often called dramatic rights)
- · Audiobooks (which may or may not be licensed with other Publication Rights)
- · Other languages, gaming, merchandising… The list goes on to as many ways as you can think of (ex. *Games of Thrones* slot machines, Star Wars branded Coca Cola cans, etc.)
- **Contract** – A legally binding document that lays out the terms for the licensing of various copyrights for use by others. (Example: first publication rights of a short story to a magazine, all publication rights in a book contract, etc.) **Quick tip:** *Licensing* isn't selling. *It is more like they're renting the right(s) for a specific period of time or some other criteria. Even though it is often called selling, make sure the contract doesn't say that.*

- **Reversion of Rights** – This is getting the rights *back* that have been licensed by contract to a publisher for that certain period of time or other criteria (such as until the number of copies sold per year falls below a contractually agreed minimum). Once a right is reverted, it may be reused, repackaged, licensed to someone else, etc.

- **Distributor** – A distributor is different from a publisher. (Think Amazon, Barnes and Noble, Kobo, etc.) What they do is have a "Terms of Services" agreement (you know about TOSs, they're the long annoying things that you click

"I Accept" without reading them so that you can install something). These typically state that for the "non-exclusive right" to distribute your work, they get to keep a percentage of every sale. Non-exclusive means that they can distribute it, but are taking no other rights, not even the sole right to distribute.

- **Quasi-Distributor** – (not their real name). These are distributors who take an exclusive right, typically only for a period of time. For example, ACX offers two different contracts for publication of audio books on their site. They are actually a publisher, even though they may look like a distributor.
- **Living Trust** – This is a legal object which just means that all of the IP is bundled together so that it can be handled as a single unit, literally given *in trust* to an heir. That way it can be inherited and managed immediately without getting snarled up in Probate Court.

COPYRIGHT -a very brief introduction

The copyright represented by my body of work belongs to me, the author, and my heirs until my death plus seventy years. That means that if properly managed, the estate can be earning exclusive income for seventy years after my demise. (Is that cool or what!)

Some of that copyright may be encumbered by various contracts. I've attempted to include a copy of all relevant ones in this folder. But none of those contracts usurp the ownership of the copyright, they are only licenses to exercise some of those rights for the length of the contract. The copyright itself still belongs to me and, eventually, you, my heirs.

If allowed to go fallow, earnings from my collection of IP (Intellectual Property, the stuff I wrote) will slowly decay to zero (or near enough), because the works will sell less and less over time. If managed and maintained, the value will be significantly higher, and may even be increased over time.

This last may seem counterintuitive, but there are numerous cases where careful management has increased (sometimes drastically increased) the value of an estate based in intellectual property. Like by making movies of books, new promotions, new books by other authors under a licensing agreement, etc.

BANKRUPTCY

Whoever holds the IP (presently my spouse and I) can *never, ever* declare bankruptcy. It's just *not* an option. If we did, the court would declare the IP to be assets of the holder and confiscate them to settle debts. All of that potential income for life plus seventy years is now gone and belongs to someone else. Now that you own my IP? No bankruptcy allowed…ever!

IMPORTANT MANAGEMENT INFO

MANAGING THE TRUST

There are six ways that I can think of to do this with descending degrees of your involvement and commensurate descending income for you. Frankly, I expect anyone, except maybe my spouse, will go straight to option #3 or #5, so I'm working to make sure they're well set up.

Quick tip:

One of these is very strenuously not (I repeat: NOT) recommended, but you, my heirs, need to be aware of it to choose wisely.

1. **Manage it yourself** – high involvement, best income if you want to become highly educated in the process. I don't see anyone doing this. I mean, crap, I can barely do this.
2. **Hire fee-based services on an as-needed basis** – You remain highly involved in the direction of the work, but you hire out the work itself to fee-based companies (this many dollars for a new cover, this much to load it to

a new distributor, etc.). This is actually what I do now: hiring out cover design, copyediting, and proofreading.

3. [*My Publishing Corporation, Inc.*] hires a publisher (part- or full-time).

   · This would be a paid employee responsible for managing the trust I mentioned above. Make sure an employment contract is in place that specifies that there is no implied right to company-managed IP.

   · You would meet with them, approve their recommendations (at least in a general way), *and always write the checks yourself.*

   · This is a highly viable option. For recommendations, consult with:

     - *List of key publishing friends with their contact info (and get their agreement first).*

   · I like this solution a lot. Hire a person or a company with a statement something like: "Here are all of his files and login passwords. I will pay you $5,000 per year (or whatever, depending upon amount of income the estate itself generates—think 5-10% of gross income as a guideline). I want you to do everything you can to increase the estate for that fee. Refresh covers, pub into new markets and technologies, commission audio, get into film, etc." The biggest benefits to this entire scenario are that you keep all of the rights, most of the money, and your main decision is whom to hire—then hands off.

- You can also pay them the way salespeople are paid: base plus commission. That is: a smaller base salary plus a percentage of the profits they make over a certain amount each year.

· If the results hold strong or climb, contract with them for another year—at the same percentage of gross income as an enticement. If the results fall off (especially drastic fall-off), then find another person or company the next year and try again.

· If this were to happen tomorrow, I would suggest calling my friends and asking for recommendations:

- [*List of key publishing friends with their contact info*].

4. **Hire a share-based manager** – ICK! This is effectively giving away the controls of the IP and giving them a share of copyright for life plus seventy years. There are going to be a ton of scams in this area, including some already run by present-day agents. A lot of people will try to talk you into doing this one. Protect yourself...DON'T!

Quick tip:

There are a few reputable presses working to fill this gap. If you go this way, limit the length of copyright as much as possible (Ex: three years with right to renew on mutually agreeable terms).

5. **Give away management of the trust to a reputable beneficiary (in exchange for a percentage of income).** This is not as unreal as it sounds. It is the most hands-off way to do this, but probably the lowest income one.

- The will includes the suggestion of giving it to [*My College*] Writing Department. I intend to do further work to make sure this is a viable and prepared option. The idea is that they, or someone else like the American Red Cross or my state's Public Broadcasting, would manage the estate to their own benefit and then pay you a check of 50% of the income, or something like that. You may make less, but it *is* hassle-free.
- Cashing the check would be your only contact with them. But retain the rights to manage the overall block of IP itself, even if someone else is managing the IP. That way, if they're doing a crappy job after two, three, or five years, you can pull the trust and give it to some other charity that you think will manage it better.

Quick tips:

- In all of these (except possibly the last one), you should have your own CPA.
- You should hire an IP lawyer to look at any agreement you make contractually; they're expensive but worth it.

- Do whatever you can to make it so that you write the checks and you deposit the income. *Only you* ever write the checks and deposit the income. Options #1-#3 all allow for you to do this.

OTHER VARIATIONS ON THE THEME

1. To keep the IP fresh, if there is a big following in a particular series, there is the possibility of hiring a writer to continue the series. Historically look at Brandon Sanderson being contracted to complete *The Wheel of Time* after the author Robert Jordan's death. There would have to be a negotiated contract as to how the IP and income are managed. However, even if very little direct income is generated for the estate, it would have the advantage of pumping new reader interest and energy into the series.

2. The IP could actually be sold rather than licensed. I don't think this is advisable, but it is an option. Let's say a block of IP is generating $XX/year. It might be sold to a corporation (Example: Disney buying Star Wars and Marvel), for a one-time lump sum. That sum must be worth it to you, the heir, to forego all future income.

3. There is an option to give it all away, to turn everything into the public domain (free to

the public for enjoyment, use, or reuse) via a Creative Commons license. As this is giving away *all* future money and control, I wouldn't do this under any circumstances; but it is an option to be aware of.

MY PUBLISHING CORPORATION, INC.

This is a [state]-based corporation that has an auto-renewing year-to-year right to manage, publish, and promote my Intellectual Property. Note: It does NOT own my IP. That is owned by me as a person and will end up in my trust. It may be that [*My Corp, Inc.*] will be the best way to manage the on-going IP (for example under option #2 or #3, [*My Corp, Inc.*] would hire the publisher or the management company). However, if you give away the trust as in Option #5 above, then you will want to check with a CPA on whether or not the corporation serves any on-going purpose or should be dissolved.

[*My Corp, Inc.'s*] current CPA is:
   [*Contact information*]

WHERE'S THE MONEY?

BANK ACCOUNTS

There are presently six checking/savings accounts. (Checkbooks are typically kept at this location…)

- [*Bank YYY*] (checking) – this is the Internet and Direct Deposit account. We call it a "sweep" or "Internet" account. The idea is that everyone like Amazon, Barnes & Noble, etc. are set up to directly deposit into this account. We write a check any time the account crosses $1,000 to drop the balance back to a $500 baseline. We then hand carry it to [*Bank ZZZ*], where it is deposited in Corporate Checking. What this does is makes it so that the [*Bank YYY*] routing and account number that is out there in the world, that could potentially be used to *remove* money from this account, can't ever be taken for very much. It is like a financial firewall. (If big Hollywood money ever comes in, you want to be prepared to move it within the hour. Trust me on that.)
- [*Bank ZZZ*] ([*My Corp Inc.'s*] checking/savings) – this is the corporation's checking and savings account.
- [*Bank ZZZ*] (Personal checking/savings) – this is our personal checking and savings account. Quick tip: *A corporation is a separate*

tax entity from a person. Therefore, you can never co-mingle funds. Ex: Using a corporate card to pay for groceries is a huge no-no with ugly tax and legal consequences. Money may only be moved across as a corporate "draw to shareholders" or a salary (plus a few odd exceptions, but talk to a CPA before attempting any of this).

- [*Bank ZZZ*] (Personal "big" or "long-term" savings) – this is a separate account with a higher yield rate.
- [*Broker ZZZ*] (Investment accounts)

WHERE'SMONEY TRACKED?

The money is tracked in two separate programs, both on my computer.

- Quicken is used to track all personal income and expenses. This is essential information for preparing personal taxes. (Quick tip: Think of it as a fancy checkbook with everything filed by categories and you'll be fine.)
- Quickbooks is used for all [*My Corp Inc.*] accounting. This is a more powerful and complex tool. In addition to being the corporate checkbook, it can be used to issue paychecks to employees, pay federal and state corporate taxes, and shareholder draws. You can give this data file to a CPA if you hire one

to handle all of your accounting and taxes for you. (You should still be the one signing the checks!)

HOW IN THE *HELL* DO I USE ALL OF THIS SOFTWARE?

I have a series of step-by-step "how to" guides stored on my computer. They list every single keystroke necessary to perform each of these tasks. Overwhelming at first and more than a little daunting even once you know how it works.

So what do you do?

1. You can try tackling it yourself. (Oy! Royal pain in the butt, just warning you. There are federal, state, and, depending on where you live or keep the corporation, Local taxes and they have to be filed at certain times.)

2. There are third-party payroll processing companies (like ADP and Quickbooks) who will do the payroll portion (which is the really tricky bit) for you, for a fee. Probably well worth it.

3. You can hire an accountant to do it all for you. In this case, you would meet with the accountant and then probably just hand them the Quickbooks file. (**Quick tip:** You will still want to authorize and sign *every single* check yourself so that you know what's

happening to your money. Can't repeat that one enough.)

An accountant can absolutely help you decide between options #2 and #3 and help you get set up.

PERSONAL MONEY

In addition to the bank accounts, there is other personal money. At the moment this includes:

- [*List of various retirement investment accounts*]

Records for these may be found clearly filed in the big file cabinet.

Other personal money matters (credit cards, utilities, rent, etc.) are outside of the scope of this document but may all be found filed in the same cabinet.

Back-year information:

- We maintain the last seven years of bills and statements, filed by year, stored in separate folders in the large plastic bin.
- Every tax filing (going way back) is in the plastic crate sitting on the bookshelf.

WHERE'S THE MONEY COMING FROM?

CONTRACTUAL ROYALTIES

As of this writing, I have books contracted as noted below. They should be sending regular royalty statements through the regular mail with checks or as direct deposit (with online statements that can be found *here* and *here).* If you have not received them by the dates noted, contact the publisher:

- [*Trad. Publisher A*] – the following list of books (royalty statements due: *May 10* and *November 10 at the latest—call if you don't get them)*
- [*Audio Publisher*] – [*these books*]
- [*Film or TV...etc.*]

There may also be one-time royalties arriving from magazine or anthology publishers (sometimes paid on date of purchase, but more often paid on date of publication). Each one should be reflected in the contracts file in the file cabinet.

OTHER CASH STREAMS

In the independent publishing world there are a wide variety of cash streams. The more successful

I get, the more numerous they become. Almost all of ours are directed into the "sweep / Internet" account noted above, so that they should be easy to manage. Here's the current list of who you should expect regular monthly payments from (some will have multiple deposits for the same vendor (Ex: Amazon for each major country):

- Amazon
- Apple iBooks
- Barnes & Noble
- Draft2Digital
- Kobo
- *Etc.*

In addition to these, some few vendors will deposit to PayPal (or Amazon Payments, ApplePay, StoryBundle, etc). This money may accumulate in that online account until you manually move it into the sweep / Internet bank account using the password information in the Password file noted below. Reminder: This is corporate income and should *never* be mixed with your personal PayPal account.

INFORMATION NEEDED BY WHOEVER IS MANAGING THE ACTUAL STUFF I'VE WRITTEN

OTHER FILES IN THIS DIRECTORY

You, my heir, don't necessarily need to understand all of these documents, but you will need to get them to the publisher you hire or whoever is going to manage the on-going copyrights.

- Contracts
  - Short story contracts—these only affect the restriction of copyright for a brief period of time. (Ex: [*ZZZ Magazine*] holds exclusive rights until 60 days after publication. After that, they retain the rights to on-going non-exclusive reprints, but all other rights revert to the copyright holder.)
  - Traditional contracts—The publishers have been granted the right to exclusively exercise most of the rights (but not movies or translations). There are several ways, over time, to recover these rights, which will be detailed in "Reversion of Rights" below. The goal is to get all of the rights back eventually so that they can then be refreshed and relicensed in profitable ways.
- *Publishing the Book.xls:* This is the master

file to all of my works—every single title is represented here. All key information can be used to track each title and also track any action that needs to be taken in the future to get the licensed rights back, etc. *Publishing the Book.xls* includes:

· Name of every title published (novel, short story, non-fiction…all there)
· ISBN of print publications
· Date of publication
· What channels (distributors like Amazon, B&N, etc.) it has been published in
· Whether it has been filed with the Library of Congress through the US Copyright Office
· There is a lot of other information, but those are the main pieces

• *PW.xls:* This is the master password file. (Note: this file is locked with a password that will be given orally, or it is in my safety deposit box, or it is filed with the law firm of [*YYY*].)

· This includes the current passwords to access all accounts including:
  - Distributors (Amazon, Apple, Barnes & Noble, Kobo, etc.)
  - Website (***Quick tip:*** don't let the website domain names or the website hosting lapse. I receive invoice emails, and renewal dates can be viewed on the ISP/host's site as well. Presently with [*ZZZhost*].)
  - Email
  - PayPal

- Social Media
- And everything else

FILES *NOT* IN THIS DIRECTORY (but important)

All files exist in 3 locations at the time of this writing.

- On my laptop.
- The daily backup I carry in my pocket.
- The weekly backup that goes in [*this place off-site*].

Directory structures:

The first four main folders are what a publisher or company will need [see "Managing the Trust" above] in order to work with the books, short stories, etc. You don't care about these...but the publisher/technician you hire will be thrilled. The second to last one is about running the business itself:

- A-Books
- Series
  - Title
    - Finished files (including files that actually get uploaded to the distributors, etc.).
    - Master working InDesign files
    - Cover folder

- · Finished covers
- · Working folder including InDesign & image files
- - Archive / reference folder
- - Old documents, prior versions etc.
- - iTunes Package (itmsp): These are the files that a technical person will need to update books uploaded to iBooks with iTunes Producer
- - Vellum, Scrivener, InDesign, or other layout file: these files are the interior layout files for the title
- - Key file: This is a simple Word file that contains all of the information needed about each title including:
  - · Subject categories
  - · Keywords
  - · Short blurb
  - · Full blurb
  - · Reviews (very handy when planning marketing)
- A-Short Stories
  - · Similar structure to books
  - · Collections
    - - Yearly collection of short fiction (from my monthly free short story).
  - · Short stories – old and dead
    - - Probably none good enough to unearth. Old crap I couldn't face deleting.
  - · Works in Progress
    - - These are typically works in process, or

they're under contract and will be published after the rights revert back to me.

- A-Images as purchased folder
  - This contains every image used on the front and back covers of books that I have purchased the right to use, and a copy of the license.
- B-Audio Projects
  - The audio files that I have made or had made of various works. These are primarily loaded through ACX, a "quasi"-distributor as mentioned above.
- B-Business
  - Everything on the business side from IRS communications, contracts to [*My Corporation, Inc.*] corporation documents, meeting minutes, etc.
- B-Other Writing
  - Mostly classes I've given and notes on ones I've taken.

ONE LAST NOTE

REVERSION OF RIGHTS

Copyrights may be licensed by contracts (Ex: [*my traditional publisher*]) that include publication and other rights. Or there are also simpler licenses for just distribution rights (Ex:

Amazon, Kobo, B&N, Apple, etc). Most of the latter may be canceled by going into the distribution channel and simply removing the book from publication. Some of the latter (Ex: ACX) are covered by more restrictive contracts that include a time-frame for cancellation.

The rest of this section is about Reversion of Rights when more rights than "simple distribution" are involved (Example: the actual copyright licensed to publish a book).

At present, this includes all of the [*YYY Publisher*] titles.

A Reversion of Rights means that the contracted licensee will no longer have the right to distribute a work once it is reverted. There are two primary ways this can happen:

1. **Contractual Limitations** – Every contract should have (all mine do) a Reversion of Rights clause. This sets the criteria for the reversion.

   · *Anthology A*: All rights, except for on-going reprints as an anthology, revert after 60 days. This happens automatically.

   · *Traditional Publisher B*: Reversion of rights may be requested per the terms of the contract, when a threshold is met (for example, number of books sold per year falls below a minimum). There are things they can do to block the reversion and there are times to hire an attorney to fight those blocks.

2. **Rights may be bought back** – If a title is selling relatively slowly, consider giving the publisher an offer they can't refuse to buy back the rights. Then you can republish (possibly independently). (Example letter to the publisher: "At your current rate of sales, you can expect to make $[XX] over the next 10 years. I would like to offer that to you as a lump sum for the re-purchase of my rights.") This probably won't be possible in the first 5-10 years of publication, but is a very real possibility after that.

3. **35-Year Rule** – This one is Copyright Law. Here are the very basics, again an attorney can help. The Nolo Press *Copyright Handbook* has a very useful section on this as well. It essentially goes like this:

   · 30-34 years after contract date (as noted in *Publishing the Book.xls)* a notice *must* be sent to the US Copyright Office requesting reversion.

   · At 35 years your rights revert, you then notify the publisher.

   · You can choose to relicense that copyright for a hefty fee.

   · You can take ownership, send take-down notices to the publisher, and republish the book in a different channel (whatever it may be at that future date). All rights will return to the trust so that you can do this.

   (end of Final Letter)

Final Letter – Last Thoughts

That is the generic draft of my Final Letter. It provides education and guidance, with*out* instruction, in English (mostly). I wrote this and walked each of my heirs through it (it only took about an hour each). They were thrilled at the explanation; for them it had been an enormous and scary burden until that moment.

As anyone who manages IP knows, it is never this simple. But this letter gives them a basic understanding and a plan of attack. I feel that it was the single best step toward protecting my legacy that I've ever made. And in protecting that legacy, I am also doing the very best thing to protect my heirs.

PART VII: A Plan of Action

This section is to help you know where to begin and a few final thoughts.

The Final Package

Earlier I mentioned The Final Package as distinct from the Final Letter. Once every quarter or so, I send a complete package to all of the potential executors. I tell them not to bother with it until I die. Then it will become very important.

It includes:

- The most recent copy of the will and trust documents.
- The most recent copy of my passwords file (or instructions on where to find it).
- The most recent copy of my Publishing the Book file.

- The most recent copy of The Final Letter. That is why I placed a revision date at the top of the letter. I make very few changes here, except for the names of professionals (writers, accountant, lawyers).

The only real change to this Final Package is the updates to my master IP file: *PublishingTheBook. xls.* The Will and the Final Letter may go years between changes. But I send them anyway so that they are consistently in one easy-to-access place. If you go all of the way back to my list of directories in Part IV: Organizing It All, you will also see that it is prominently listed in the Business folder > Estate Planning; right where an executor is most likely to stumble on it.

Educating the Heir

At least once, you want to sit down with each heir and executor and walk them through the Final Letter. More often is better.

But by walking them through at least once, they will hopefully understand that this isn't just something "crazy old Matt used to do for fun" or "this thing is so huge I just can't deal with it." You want them to understand that there is potentially a long-term legacy here that they can take advantage of…someday.

Getting From Where You Are—To There

This is my recommended method if you are approaching this from scratch.

1. Make a will that is current and addresses IP – This is the essential first step.
2. Educate your heir(s) in the basics – Start out with this right away, just in case you don't get around to the other stuff before it's too late. Or at least hand them a copy of this book.
3. Make an ugly draft of The Final Letter – Review it with the heir. Incorporate answers to their questions in next draft.
4. Organize the money
5. Organize your IP
6. Make a better draft of The Final Letter
7. Research living trusts
8. Update The Final Letter quarterly
   · Even if it's just your Master IP file
   · Review letter annually yourself to make sure that all of the contact information is correct
9. Reeducate your heir

Now you will have built a very solid basis so that your written legacy will survive and provide on-going support or even livelihood for the heirs of your choice.

PART VIII: Suggested Reading (for the author, not so much for the heir)

- *LLC or Corporation?* by Anthony Mancuso (Nolo Press)
- *Tax Savvy for Small Businesses* by Frederick W. Daily (Nolo Press)
- *Deduct It!* by Stephen Fishman (Nolo Press) – less useful, but a good backup reference
- *The Copyright Handbook* by Stephen Fishman (Nolo Press)
- *Plan Your Estate* by Denis Clifford (Nolo Press)
- *Make Your Own Living Trust* by Denis Clifford (Nolo Press)
- *Estate Planning for Authors* by Gin Jones
- *Trial and Heirs* by Mayoras and Mayoras (a great read for authors and heirs)

Even though I'm not a lawyer (nor do I play one on TV), I'm always trying to improve this book and the information in it, both for my heirs and for others. Please contact me at ml@mlbuchman.com with any thoughts or needed clarifications. I will not offer advice, legal or otherwise, about your individual situation for liability reasons, but I would love to hear from you.

About the Author

M.L. Buchman started the first of, what is now over 50 novels and as many short stories, while flying from South Korea to ride his bicycle across the Australian Outback. Part of a solo around the world trip that ultimately launched his writing career.

All three of his military romantic suspense series—The Night Stalkers, Firehawks, and Delta Force—have had a title named "Top 10 Romance of the Year" by the American Library Association's Booklist. NPR and Barnes & Noble have named other titles "Top 5 Romance of the Year." In 2016 he was a finalist for Romance Writers of America prestigious RITA award. He also writes: contemporary romance, thrillers, and fantasy.

Past lives include: years as a project manager, rebuilding and single-handing a fifty-foot sailboat, both flying and jumping out of airplanes, and he has designed and built two houses. He is now making his living as a full-time writer on the Oregon Coast with his beloved wife and is constantly amazed at what you can do with a degree in Geophysics. You may keep up with his writing and receive a free starter e-library by subscribing to his newsletter at:

www.mlbuchman.com

If you enjoyed this, you might also enjoy:

Managing Your Inner Artist/ Writer (excerpt)
-Strategies for Success #1-

PURPOSE / ORIGINS

The purpose of this work is to lay the groundwork for the artist in each of us to be nurtured. We hope to offer a practical way to allow the business of art to thrive without impinging on the creative process.

This began as a series of lectures presented to both writing and business professionals regarding the project management of an artist, especially when that artist is oneself. It has been presented to hundreds of writers covering every genre.

The authors have collaborated to create a structure and methodology (a way of thinking and a way to do things) that is accessible to every artist whether they are a writer, a photographer, a painter, or a professional sand-sculpturist (who even knew there was such a thing until we saw them specifically disbarred from a local sand-castling competition on the Oregon Coast).

WHAT THIS BOOK IS...AND ISN'T

The first lecture in this series began when Matt became overwhelmed by the problems of how to write, work to contract deadlines in traditional publishing, publish his own work in the (then) new indie-publishing, and learn all that he felt he had to learn...while working a totally insane day job.

Through a long series of experiments, both failed and successful, and wide study, we decided that the conflicts and overlaps became easier to manage when we divided our thinking into three areas:
- The craft of our art.
- The business person managing our art.
- The business of our art.

This book is intended to reside completely within the second of these three. This is not a book of craft in any field. Nor is this a book of the business side of whatever craft you practice. This is a book talking to the person who must manage both of these in any field.

Further, within that middle role, we can easily list dozens of sub-roles. These roles can all be filled by one person. (Matt's friend Scott Carter, who we'll revisit later, calls his writing career: "Running a publishing empire from my laptop.") Or these roles can be filled by many people. Each form of art will be unique, but may include common items such as:
- Education
- Educator –for often the best way to learn is to teach
- Finance
- Insurance
- Designer
- Contract specialist
- Purchasing
- Marketing...

The list feels infinite, and we have no intention of trying to address infinity (just in case it turns out that the list really is infinite, we'd rather not know). What we are going to focus on is this single, all-important task:

Managing your inner artist to the greatest success.

That success can be defined as monetary, creative, innovative, and a myriad of other ways. But the challenge we faced was: how can we best help that inner artist find their way toward your chosen goal.

This task can't be outsourced. No one can create a document and present it to your inner artist that will help them. No one can demand of the inner artist what they are unable or unwilling to give. Or that they flat out don't understand. Attempting to do so will usually cause anxiety and / or guilt, and shut down the inner artist, the last thing you want.

This role of managing and nurturing *must* be owned by the artist themselves for only they will know what works and what doesn't.

The intention of this book is to offer a tool set to aid "You the practical person" in working in a collaborative (as opposed to authoritative) manner with "You the artist."

(Available at fine retailers everywhere)

Other works by M.L. Buchman

Strategies for Success: (NF)
Manaaging Your Inner Artist / Writer
Estate Planning for Authors

Where Dreams
Where Dreams are Born
Where Dreams Reside
Where Dreams Are of Christmas
Where Dreams Unfold
Where Dreams Are Written

Eagle Cove
Return to Eagle Cove
Recipe for Eagle Cove
Longing for Eagle Cove
Keepsake for Eagle Cove

Henderson's Ranch
Nathan's Big Sky

The Night Stalkers

MAIN FLIGHT
The Night Is Mine
I Own the Dawn
Wait Until Dark
Take Over at Midnight
Light Up the Night
Bring On the Dusk
By Break of Day

WHITE HOUSE HOLIDAY
Daniel's Christmas

Don't Miss a Thing!

Sign up for M. L. Buchman's newsletter
today
and receive:
Release News
Free Short Stories
a Free Starter Library

Do it today. Do it now.
http://www.mlbuchman.com/newsletter/

Made in the USA
Middletown, DE
12 September 2021